This Journal Belongs To:

Date

Funniest Thing That Happened

Best Thing That Happened

Best Thing I Ate

Who I Shared the Day With

I'm Going to Dream About...

Date

Funniest Thing That Happened

Best Thing That Happened

Best Thing I Ate

Who I Shared the Day With

I'm Going to Dream About...

Date

Funniest Thing That Happened

Best Thing That Happened

Best Thing I Ate

Who I Shared the Day With

I'm Going to Dream About...

Date

Funniest Thing That Happened

Best Thing That Happened

Best Thing I Ate

Who I Shared the Day With

I'm Going to Dream About...

Date

Funniest Thing That Happened

Best Thing That Happened

Best Thing I Ate

Who I Shared the Day With

I'm Going to Dream About...

Date

Funniest Thing That Happened

Best Thing That Happened

Best Thing I Ate

Who I Shared the Day With

I'm Going to Dream About...

Date

Funniest Thing That Happened

Best Thing That Happened

Best Thing I Ate

Who I Shared the Day With

I'm Going to Dream About...

Date

Funniest Thing That Happened

Best Thing That Happened

Best Thing I Ate

Who I Shared the Day With

I'm Going to Dream About...

Date

Funniest Thing That Happened

Best Thing That Happened

Best Thing I Ate

Who I Shared the Day With

I'm Going to Dream About...

Date

Funniest Thing That Happened

Best Thing That Happened

Best Thing I Ate

Who I Shared the Day With

I'm Going to Dream About...

Date

Funniest Thing That Happened

Best Thing That Happened

Best Thing I Ate

Who I Shared the Day With

I'm Going to Dream About...

Date

Funniest Thing That Happened

Best Thing That Happened

Best Thing I Ate

Who I Shared the Day With

I'm Going to Dream About...

Date

Funniest Thing That Happened

Best Thing That Happened

Best Thing I Ate

Who I Shared the Day With

I'm Going to Dream About...

Date

Funniest Thing That Happened

Best Thing That Happened

Best Thing I Ate

Who I Shared the Day With

I'm Going to Dream About...

Date

Funniest Thing That Happened

Best Thing That Happened

Best Thing I Ate

Who I Shared the Day With

I'm Going to Dream About...

Date

Funniest Thing That Happened

Best Thing That Happened

Best Thing I Ate

Who I Shared the Day With

I'm Going to Dream About...

Date

Funniest Thing That Happened

Best Thing That Happened

Best Thing I Ate

Who I Shared the Day With

I'm Going to Dream About...

Date

Funniest Thing That Happened

Best Thing That Happened

Best Thing I Ate

Who I Shared the Day With

I'm Going to Dream About...

Date

Funniest Thing That Happened

Best Thing That Happened

Best Thing I Ate

Who I Shared the Day With

I'm Going to Dream About...

Date

Funniest Thing That Happened

Best Thing That Happened

Best Thing I Ate

Who I Shared the Day With

I'm Going to Dream About...

Date

Funniest Thing That Happened

Best Thing That Happened

Best Thing I Ate

Who I Shared the Day With

I'm Going to Dream About...

Date

Funniest Thing That Happened

Best Thing That Happened

Best Thing I Ate

Who I Shared the Day With

I'm Going to Dream About...

Date

Funniest Thing That Happened

Best Thing That Happened

Best Thing I Ate

Who I Shared the Day With

I'm Going to Dream About...

Date

Funniest Thing That Happened

Best Thing That Happened

Best Thing I Ate

Who I Shared the Day With

I'm Going to Dream About...

Date

Funniest Thing That Happened

Best Thing That Happened

Best Thing I Ate

Who I Shared the Day With

I'm Going to Dream About...

Date

Funniest Thing That Happened

Best Thing That Happened

Best Thing I Ate

Who I Shared the Day With

I'm Going to Dream About...

Date

Funniest Thing That Happened

Best Thing That Happened

Best Thing I Ate

Who I Shared the Day With

I'm Going to Dream About...

Date

Funniest Thing That Happened

Best Thing That Happened

Best Thing I Ate

Who I Shared the Day With

I'm Going to Dream About...

Date

Funniest Thing That Happened

Best Thing That Happened

Best Thing I Ate

Who I Shared the Day With

I'm Going to Dream About...

Date

Funniest Thing That Happened

Best Thing That Happened

Best Thing I Ate

Who I Shared the Day With

I'm Going to Dream About...

Date

Funniest Thing That Happened

Best Thing That Happened

Best Thing I Ate

Who I Shared the Day With

I'm Going to Dream About...

Date

Funniest Thing That Happened

Best Thing That Happened

Best Thing I Ate

Who I Shared the Day With

I'm Going to Dream About...

Date

Funniest Thing That Happened

Best Thing That Happened

Best Thing I Ate

Who I Shared the Day With

I'm Going to Dream About...

Date

Funniest Thing That Happened

Best Thing That Happened

Best Thing I Ate

Who I Shared the Day With

I'm Going to Dream About...

Date

Funniest Thing That Happened

Best Thing That Happened

Best Thing I Ate

Who I Shared the Day With

I'm Going to Dream About...

Date

Funniest Thing That Happened

Best Thing That Happened

Best Thing I Ate

Who I Shared the Day With

I'm Going to Dream About...

Date

Funniest Thing That Happened

Best Thing That Happened

Best Thing I Ate

Who I Shared the Day With

I'm Going to Dream About...

Date

Funniest Thing That Happened

Best Thing That Happened

Best Thing I Ate

Who I Shared the Day With

I'm Going to Dream About...

Date

Funniest Thing That Happened

Best Thing That Happened

Best Thing I Ate

Who I Shared the Day With

I'm Going to Dream About...

Date

Funniest Thing That Happened

Best Thing That Happened

Best Thing I Ate

Who I Shared the Day With

I'm Going to Dream About...

Date

Funniest Thing That Happened

Best Thing That Happened

Best Thing I Ate

Who I Shared the Day With

I'm Going to Dream About...

Date

Funniest Thing That Happened

Best Thing That Happened

Best Thing I Ate

Who I Shared the Day With

I'm Going to Dream About...

Date

Funniest Thing That Happened

Best Thing That Happened

Best Thing I Ate

Who I Shared the Day With

I'm Going to Dream About…

Date

Funniest Thing That Happened

Best Thing That Happened

Best Thing I Ate

Who I Shared the Day With

I'm Going to Dream About...

Date

Funniest Thing That Happened

Best Thing That Happened

Best Thing I Ate

Who I Shared the Day With

I'm Going to Dream About...

Date

Funniest Thing That Happened

Best Thing That Happened

Best Thing I Ate

Who I Shared the Day With

I'm Going to Dream About...

Date

Funniest Thing That Happened

Best Thing That Happened

Best Thing I Ate

Who I Shared the Day With

I'm Going to Dream About...

Made in the USA
Coppell, TX
15 May 2021

55567290R10057